Explosive Combat
Wing Chun

Volume Two

EXPLOSIVE COMBAT
WING CHUN

Volume Two

SIFU ALAN LAMB

UNIQUE PUBLICATIONS
Burbank, California

Disclaimer
Please note that the author and publisher of this book are NOT RESPONSIBLE in any manner whatsoever for any injury that may result from practicing the techniques and/or following the instructions given within. Since the physical activities described herein may be too strenuous in nature for some readers to engage in safely, it is essential that a physician be consulted prior to training.

First published in 2002 by Unique Publications.

Library of Congress Catalog Number: 2002015355
ISBN: 0-86568-209-7

Unique Publications
4201 Vanowen Place
Burbank, CA 91505
(800) 332–3330

First edition
05 04 03 02 01 00 99 98 97 1 3 5 7 9 10 8 6 4 2

Printed in the United States of America

Editor: John S. Soet
Design: Patrick Gross
Cover Design: George Chen

DEDICATION

This book is dedicated to the memory of 9-11 and the heroes of Flight 93, who had the courage to stand up and fight evil, and against all odds did the right thing. God bless America!

ACKNOWLEDGEMENTS

First, and foremost, I would like to thank Lori Abril for her tireless help and support in the preparation of this manuscript. Also, for her posing in the photographs and so aptly demonstrating the Cham Kiu or Second Wing Chun set for the readers of this book.

Thanks to Quang V. Dang, Ziv Agmon, and Chris Ashford for posing in the self-defense section of this book.

And last, but not least, to Jose M. Fraguas and the staff of C.F.W. Enterprises for their interest and support in getting this book published.

CONTENTS

FOREWORD

As a woman and a long time fan of the martial arts, I decided to study Wing Chun Kung-Fu primarily because it is practical, effective, and also because it was Bruce Lee's original system. When I attended one of Sifu Lamb's classes back in 1988, I knew immediately that the art was for me. What struck me most was Wing Chun's emphasis on skill and technique rather than brute force. Thus, I recognized Wing Chun—with its "center line" theory, emphasis on "economy of motion," and simultaneous block and strike techniques—as a "thinking" man's/woman's art.

Today, my demanding schedule of graduate studies and full-time work leaves little time for training. However, I try to keep my hand in whenever I can, and what I have found is that because I worked so hard for so many years on perfecting Wing Chun basics—as opposed to trying to rush through the system—I have been able to retain most of what I learned. Believe me, if you take the time to learn the Wing Chun forms and techniques correctly, they will stick with you.

There are many theories as to the origins of Wing Chun. However, as a woman and a romantic I like the legend of Yim Wing Chun and the concept that Wing Chun was developed by a woman. All I can say is that from a woman's perspective, Wing Chun seems to "fit" a woman better than any other art I have seen, which leads me to conclude that if Wing Chun was not created by women, then they certainly played a major role in its development.

As the events of the past year have demonstrated, we live in troubled times and no one is safe either from personal attack or acts of terrorism. Therefore, I encourage people everywhere, especially women, to take personal responsibility for their safety and learn some form of the martial arts to protect themselves. If Wing Chun classes are not available in your area, any martial arts class taught by a responsible, certified instructor would be a wise investment of your time.

Whatever level of martial arts training you are at, I believe you will find this book of value, and I hope you get as much out of it as we did putting it together.

—Lori Abril

Introduction

I would like to thank you all for purchasing this copy of *Explosive Combat Wing Chun*—Volume 2. I have long wanted to produce a book containing all three of Wing Chun's basic empty hand sets: The "Siu Lum Tau," which means the "nucleus" or "small idea" set, the "Cham Kiu," which means "sinking" or "searching for the bridge" set, and "Biu Jee," which can mean "thrusting" or "flying fingers" set. I believe that this is the first time that all three sets have been presented together in one volume. I hope you find it a valuable addition to your Wing Chun library.

The Chinese believe that martial arts training falls into three distinct phases, which relates directly to the way in which the Wing Chun sets have been developed.

For example, phase one training—which relates to the Siu Lum Tau—usually involves some form of "Chi Gong or "energy building" exercises. It can also include stance work, endurance, and strength training.

Phase two training—which relates to Cham Kiu—usually combines exercises that facilitate the releasing of "Fa Ging," or kinetic energy. Therefore, phase two combines static and fluid motions and the object is to develop explosiveness and fluidity.

Phase three training—which relates to Biu Jee—synthesizes phase one and phase two training concepts, and works toward developing fighting or self-defense techniques or tactics.

When working through the Wing Chun sets it is important to keep this comprehensive view in mind. When you recognize that the three phases relate directly to the three sets, you will be able to develop a deeper understanding of the Wing Chun system.

Finally, I would like to add that in order to make this work accessible to all martial artists, the publishers have requested that the descriptions of all the movements be written in English, and that I keep the Chinese terminology to a minimum. Therefore, although it would be easier to use Chinese terms such as Lap Sau or Pak Sau we will use such terms sparingly and instead will describe the action as "Grabbing Hand" drill or "Slapping Hand" drill, etc. Thus, although all Wing Chun students will recognize the techniques and will probably know the Chinese terms equated with them, all those not familiar with Wing Chun should be able to fully understand the descriptions.

Anyone interested in contacting me can do so through the publisher or by writing to:

Alan Lamb's Wing Chun
1147 E. Broadway, P.M.B. #275
Glendale, CA 91205

SECTION ONE

SIU LUM TAU

INTRODUCTION TO SECTION ONE
SIU LUM TAU

The "Siu Lum Tau," which translates as "nucleus" or "small idea" set, can be considered the most important set in Wing Chun Kung-Fu. It is through the Siu Lum Tau set that all structural concepts are learned. The correct angles of attack and defense, elbow position, stance work, and breath control are just some of the skills developed through regular practice of the Siu Lum Tau set, which can be broken down into three sections.

The first section is called "Sam By Fat" or "worship Buddha three times" because the three bent wrist blocks performed in this part of the set transition into the single "prayer hand" position, which symbolically represents the worship of Buddha. The first section is concerned with stance building, elbow position, and breath control. The concept of a strong stance is fundamental to all styles of Kung-Fu. The Chinese equate the human body to a house which, without a good foundation, will collapse during a storm. Similarly, without a strong stance–strong legs and a good "root"–the structure will collapse during a fight, and all hand techniques will be ineffectual. Additionally, a correct stance is necessary to enhance abdominal support and breath control. Proper support from the legs allows one to focus the breath into the lower abdomen. From the abdomen, strength can be generated into the hips, back and arms. This will allow for a fluid release of energy into the hands, which leads into the second section of the set.

The second section of the set, is sometimes called the "Fa Ging" or "releasing energy" phase, because it teaches one how to release smoothly the energy that is built up in the first part of the set. This releasing of energy is emphasized especially through the execution of the "pressing palms" and "sweeping" knife hand strike techniques, which allows one to develop tricep power while relaxing the antagonistic bicep muscle for maximum striking effect.

Section three of the Siu Lum Tau set focuses on the correct angles of the more practical techniques for self-defense, as well as the fluid transitioning between the moves. Staying relaxed and being fluid until the exact point of impact is extremely important for effective blocking and striking. Therefore, great emphasis is placed on learning how to transition smoothly from technique to technique—the goal being to relax during transition and tense only at the point of impact.

Siu Lum Tau Set #1

◁ Assume the ready position with your feet together and your hands resting on the thighs. Exhale and place the tip of your tongue on the soft palate area above the front teeth.

➤ Raise both arms into the double palm-up position as you breathe in through the nose, drawing the breath down, into your lower abdomen.

◁ Bend the knees and strike backwards with both elbows as you draw the arms up into the high chambered position (fists at chest level).

➤ Turn the toes out 45° by rotating on your heels.

◄ Now turn the heels out by rotating on the balls of the feet. At the same time, tilt the pelvis forward by tensing the buttocks and contracting the adductor muscles in the legs. This forms the root or structural base for the basic Wing Chun parallel leg stance, which is maintained throughout the entire Siu Lum Tau set.

➤ Raise both arms up into the "crossed arm" double palm-up block position. Right hand in front.

◄ Snap both arms down and into the "crossed arm" downward block position, left hand on top.

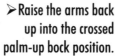

➤ Raise the arms back up into the crossed palm-up bock position.

◁ Draw both arms back into the high chambered position.

▷ Place the left fist in front of the chest (about one fist distance from the chest) on the mid-line (center line).

◁ Execute a straight line punch at nose level by locking out the elbow as you strike. Keep the shoulders down and relaxed during the punch.

▷ Open your left hand and turn it into the palm-up position.

◁ Bend the palm towards you and rotate the wrist clockwise into the "circling wrist" block.

▷ Continue circling the left hand and pause in the palm-down, knife hand position, keeping the elbow locked out.

◁ Make a fist and withdraw left hand back into the high chambered position.

▷ Now, place the right vertical fist on the mid-line, one fist distance in front of the chest.

◄ Execute a right straight punch at nose level, locking out the elbow as you strike.

➤ Open your right palm and turn it into the right side palm-up position.

◄ Bend the right palm towards you and rotate the hand counter-clockwise into the right side "circling wrist" position.

➤ Continue circling the right hand and pause in the palm-down, knife hand position.

◄ Make a fist and withdraw the right arm back into the high chambered position.

➤ Open the left hand, palm-up.

◄ Slowly push the palm forward and out so that the wrist crosses your center line.

➤ Pause in the basic palm-up block position, with the elbow placed approximately one fist and one thumb distance from the body.

◁ Bend the palm towards you and circle your left wrist clockwise.

➤ Pause, with the fingers pointing downward.

◁ Snap the fingers up as you press forward with the palm of your hand and rotate the hand into the left side single "praying hand" block.

➤ Draw the hand back slowly towards the center line and pause with the hand one fist distance from the chest.

◁ Drop the hand into the bent wrist position.

▷ Center the elbow and slowly push the arm forward, pausing when the elbow is about one fist and one thumb distance from the body.

◁ Circle the wrist clockwise, pause with the fingers pointing downward.

▷ Snap the fingers up into the "praying hand" block.

◁ Draw the hand back slowly and pause.

➤ Drop the hand into bent wrist position #2.

◁ Center the elbow and slowly push the arm forward.

➤ Circle the wrist clockwise, pause with the fingers pointing downward.

◁ Snap the fingers up into the "praying hand" block.

▷ Draw the hand back slowly and pause one fist's distance from the chest.

◁ Drop the hand into the bent wrist position #3.

▷ Draw the hand back, pause one fist's distance from the chest.

◄ Execute a "slap block" with the left palm going no further than the right shoulder.

➤ Draw the hand back to the center line.

◄ Thrust out at nose level with a vertical palm strike.

➤ Open the hand and turn it into the palm-up position.

◁ Bend the palm towards you and rotate the wrist clockwise into the "circling wrist" block.

➢ Continue circling the hand into the palm-down knife hand position.

◁ Make a fist and draw the hand back into the high chambered position.

Now repeat the same sequence of movements on the right side starting with the right hand palm-up position.

This concludes the first set of the Siu Lum Tau.

Siu Lum Tau Set #2

◄ Continuing from the high chambered position.

➤ Open the left hand and press the palm down vertically.

◄ Open the right hand and press the palm down vertically.

➤ Draw the arms up and slowly circle the arms backwards, around the waist.

◄ Pause with the backs of both palms resting on the kidney area.

➤ Strike out to the rear with both palms pressing backwards, with the fingers pointing down.

◄ (Side view of the double reverse pressing block.)

➤ Draw both arms forward and around the waist.

◁ Snap both arms forward and down into the double, "forward pressing" palms position.

▷ Raise both arms upward into the double "horizontal braced block" position—forearms in front of the chest with the palms turned downwards, left arm on top.

△ Stretch both arms out and strike to the side with both elbows.

△ Sweep out, with both palms striking to the side with an extended knife hand.

◁ Return the arms back into the horizontal braced block position, with the right arm on top.

➤ Sink both elbows down with the wrists bent, fingers pointing forward.

◁ Snap the forearms forward, blocking with the outside edge of both arms.

➤ Rotate both palms forwards and out into a double palm-up block.

◄ Sink both elbows inward to protect the center line, placing the forearms together, both palms facing downwards.

➤ Shoot both hands forward (palms facing downwards) into a double eye jab position with the fingertips

◄ Thrust both palms down into the double forward "pressing palms" position.

➤ Raise the backs of both wrists to shoulder level and into the double bent wrist block.

◄ Rotate both palms up.

➤ Make two fists and draw the arms back into the high chambered position.

This concludes the second set of the Siu Lum Tau.

Siu Lum Tau Set #3

◁ Execute a slap block with the left palm to the right shoulder and pause.

▷ Draw the palm back to the center line.

◁ Shoot forward with a left side palm strike to the head.

▷ Rotate the left palm upwards into the single palm-up position.

◁ Circle the hand clockwise and pause in the "circling wrist" block position, fingers pointing downwards.

➤ Continue circling the hand and pause in the palm-down knife hand strike position.

◁ Make a fist and withdraw the arm into the high chambered position.

➤ Execute a slap block with the right palm to the left shoulder and pause.

◁ Draw the palm back to the center line.

➤ Shoot forward with a right side palm strike to the head.

◁ Rotate the right palm upwards into the palm up position.

➤ Circle the hand counter-clockwise and pause in the "circling wrist" block, fingers pointing downwards.

◄ Continue circling the hand and pause in the palm-down knife hand strike position.

➤ Make a fist and withdraw the arm into the high chambered position.

◄ With a strong forward snapping motion, execute a left palm-up block.

➤ Sweep the arm down and into a left palm-down block.

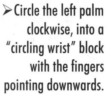 Snap the arm back up into the left palm-up block.

Circle the left palm clockwise, into a "circling wrist" block with the fingers pointing downwards.

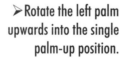 Shoot the hand forward into a left side palm strike for the body.

Rotate the left palm upwards into the single palm-up position.

◄ Circle the left palm clockwise into the "circling wrist" block with the fingers pointing downwards.

➤ Continue circling the hand and pause in the palm-down knife hand position.

◄ Make a fist and withdraw the arm into the high chambered position.

➤ With a strong forward snapping motion, execute a right palm-up block.

◄ Sweep the arm down into a right palm-down block.

➤ Snap the arm back up into the palm-up block.

◄ Circle the right palm counter-clockwise into the "circling wrist" block, fingers pointing downwards.

➤ Shoot the hand forward into a right side palm strike for the body.

◁ Rotate the right palm upwards into the single hand palm-up position.

▷ Circle the right palm counter-clockwise into a "circling wrist" block, fingers pointing downwards.

◁ Continue circling the hand and pause in the palm-down knife hand position.

▷ Make a fist and withdraw the arm into the high chambered position.

◁ Throw the left hand forward using a spiraling motion, fingers held loosely.

➤ Execute a high left hand "wing block" position.

◁ Sink the elbow down and execute a left palm-up block.

➤ Shoot the hand forward into an "inverted palm" strike, fingers pointing downwards.

◄ Rotate the left palm upwards into the single palm-up position.

➤ Circle the left palm clockwise, into a "circling wrist" block, fingers pointing downwards.

◄ Continue circling the hand and pause, in the palm-down knife hand position.

➤ Make a fist and withdraw the arm into the high chambered position.

Now repeat this same sequence of movements on the right side.

 Now sweep down with the left arm. (Sweep no. 2).

➤Sweep down with the right arm. (Sweep no. 3).

◄Sweep down with the left arm. (Sweep no. 4).

➤Now sweep down with the right arm for the final sweep. (Sweep. No. 5).

◄ Execute a left straight punch to the head. (Punch no. 1).

➤ Execute a right straight punch to the head. (Punch no. 2).

◄ Execute a left straight punch to the head. (Punch no. 3).

➤ Execute a right straight punch to the head. (Punch no. 4).

◄ Finally, execute a left straight punch to the head as you withdraw the right arm to the high chambered position. (Punch no. 5).

➤ Rotate the left palm upwards into the single palm-up position.

◄ Circle the hand clockwise and pause in the "circling wrist" block, fingers pointing downwards.

➤ Continue circling the hand and pause in the palm-down knife hand strike position.

◁ Make a fist and withdraw the left arm into the high chambered position.

➤ Draw the left foot to the right, keeping both knees bent.

◁ Release the tongue from the soft palate, exhale through the mouth, and press downwards with both palms as you straighten the legs.

➤ Step out with the left foot into a relaxed "ready" position.

This concludes the third set of the Siu Lum Tau, and completes the Siu Lum Tau section.

Section Two

Cham Kiu

INTRODUCTION TO SECTION TWO
CHAM KIU

In Cantonese "Cham Kiu" can mean "seeking" the bridge or "sinking" the bridge. The translation "seeking" applies to the "contact" aspect of Wing Chun combat. It focuses on engaging an opponent's arms through "asking hands" techniques. "Asking hands" refers to asking to receive the attacker's arms, energy, or bridge so that you can effectively "answer" the opponent's attack—"answer" being to deflect the opponent's energy and respond with the correct counter-attack. "Sinking" refers to sinking the elbow during the "Grabbing Hand" phase where the opponent's bridge is momentarily controlled as you counterattack.

As well as further developing the concept of "energy releasing," the Cham Kiu set stresses correct blocking and bridging techniques. Therefore, Cham Kiu is the model for all basic blocking drills, including Lap Sau or "Grabbing Hand" drill and Pak Sau or "Slapping Hand" drill, which also includes basic trapping techniques as fully demonstrated in Volume 1 of *Explosive Combat Wing Chun*.

Regular practice of the Cham Kiu set and associated bridging exercises leads one into the "combat" phase of Wing Chun which is further developed through practice of the Biu Jee set, Wing Chun's third form.

Cham Kiu Set—Performed by Lori Abril

◁Assume the "ready" position with the feet together.

➤Inhale as you raise your arms into the double palm-up block. At the same time, place the tip of the tongue on the soft palate area above the front teeth.

◁Bend the knees and sink the breath into the lower abdomen, then continue to breathe naturally.

➤Turn the toes out approximately 45°.

◄ Now turn the heels out, tilt the pelvis forward and "root" yourself by sinking down and into the basic Wing Chun parallel leg stance.

➤ Raise both arms up and into the "crossed arm" block, right arm in front.

◄ Snap the arms down into the "crossed arm" downward block position, left hand on top.

➤ Raise the arms back up and into the "crossed arm" block, right arm in front.

◁ Draw both arms back into the high chambered position, fists held at chest level.

➤ Place the left fist one fist's distance in front of the chest on the midline.

◁ Execute a straight left punch, elbow locked out.

➤ Turn the left hand into the palm-up position.

◄ Rotate the wrist clockwise into the "circling wrist" block.

➤ Continue circling the hand and pause, in the left palm-down knife hand position.

◄ Make a fist and draw the left arm back into the high chambered position.

Now repeat this same sequence of movements on the right side.

◁ Place both hands about a fist and a thumb's distance from the chest in a double "prayer hand" position.

➤ Strike out (at eye level) using both thumbs.

◁ Rotate the body 90° to the left by turning on the heels. Place the arms into the double "horizontal block" position with the left hand on top.

▷ Turn the body 180° to the right without changing the hand position.

◁ With a strong hip motion, rotate the body back to the left side.

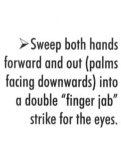

▷ Sweep both hands forward and out (palms facing downwards) into a double "finger jab" strike for the eyes.

◀ Rotate the hands into the palm-up position and sink the elbows.

➤ With a strong "push-pull" motion, snap the left palm upwards as you simultaneously slide the right palm down the left forearm, pausing at the elbow, in the "elbow break" position.

◀ Now, snap the right palm upwards as you pull down with the left palm.

➤ Repeat the movement on the left by snapping the left palm upwards as you pull down with the right.

◁ Press forward and down with the left palm.

➤ Simultaneously execute a right vertical palm strike as you withdraw the left hand into guarding position.

◁ Execute a left vertical palm strike as the right hand withdraws into guarding position.

➤ Execute a right vertical palm strike and draw the left arm back into the high chambered position.

◁ Rotate the right palm upwards.

➢ Turn towards the right, transition through the parallel stance and execute a right "horizontal block."

◁ Turn fully to the right and pause.

➢ Rotate the left palm up, in front of the chest.

◁ Turn 180° to the left as you execute a right "wing block" with the left hand placed in guarding position.

➤ Rotate both palms towards you, arms crossed, with the left hand on top.

◁ Turn right and withdraw the left arm as you execute a right "horizontal block."

➤ Turn left, execute a right "wing block."

◁ Rotate palms towards you.

➤ Turn right, execute a right "horizontal block."

◁ Rotate the left palm up.

➤ Turn left, execute a right "wing block."

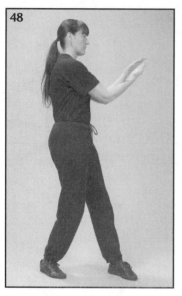

◄ Rotate palms towards you.

➤ Turn right, execute a right "horizontal block."

◄ Place the left fist on the crook of the right forearm.

➤ Sink the right elbow down and execute a "grabbing hand" block.

◀ Rotate the right palm up.

➤ Withdraw the right arm and execute a straight left punch.

◀ Rotate the left palm up.

➤ Transition back into the parallel position and execute a left "horizontal block."

◁ Sweep the left arm out to the side into a horizontal palm strike.

➤ Press forward and down with the left hand in the "pressing palm" block.

◁ Place the right hand palm-up above the left elbow.

➤ Sweep the right arm down and draw the left arm back into the high chambered position.

◁ Turn the right hand palm-up.

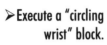

➢ Execute a "circling wrist" block.

◁ Continue to circle and wrist and pause in the knife hand block position.

➢ Make a fist and withdraw the right arm back into the high chambered position.

Now repeat this same sequence of movements on the right side.

◁Rotate the left hand, palm up on the midline.

➤Turn left into a left "horizontal block" position.

◄ Raise the left knee and execute a front "heel kick" to the body.

➤ Slide into a left forward stance and execute a right "wing block."

◄ Sink the elbows and rest the left forearm on top of the right forearm.

➤ Slide forward into a right "wing block."

◄ Sink the elbows and rest the left forearm on top of the right forearm.

➤ Slide forward into a right "wing block."

◄ Execute a right uppercut punch as you draw back the left hand.

➤ Turn back into a parallel stance and bend the right wrist, fingers pointing forwards.

◁ Snap the arm into a downward "forearm block."

➤ Place the back of the left hand on the right forearm.

◁ Execute a knife hand strike to the throat.

➤ Turn the left hand palm up.

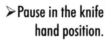 Execute the "circling wrist" block.

➢ Pause in the knife hand position.

◄ Draw the left arm back into the high chambered position.

Now repeat this same sequence of movements on the right side.

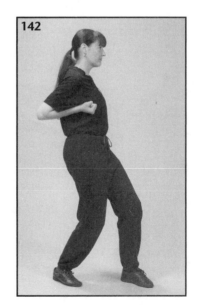

◄Execute a left front "heel kick."

►Slide into a left forward stance and execute a low double hand "wing block."

◄Sink both elbows into a double parallel palm-up block.

►Slide forward and execute a double "wing block."

◄ Sink the elbows into a double parallel palm-up block.

➤ Slide forward, double "wing block."

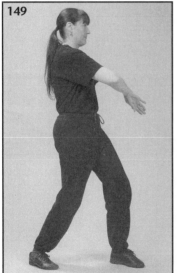

◄ Advance the left foot forward.

➤ Draw the right foot up even with the left foot. Position should be both feet together, with knees bent.

◁ Pull both arms down into a "dragging" wrist block.

➤ Straighten the legs and execute a double vertical palm strike to the body.

◁ Roll the arms and transition into a double "wing block."

➤ Bend the knees and strike to the rear with both elbows.

◁ Step backwards onto the ball of the right foot.

◁ Turn 180° to your right.

Now repeat this same sequence of movements on the right side.

◄Pivot on the ball of the right foot.

➤Turn left, and execute an outside leg block.

◄Extend into a left heel kick.

➤Pivot right and press down with the left palm.

◄ Pivot left, right palm press.

➤ Pivot right, left palm press.

◄ Pivot left, right palm press.

➤ Execute a right extension punch.

◁ Pivot right,
left palm press.

➤ Left extension
punch.

◁ Pivot left,
right palm press.

➤ Right extension
punch.

◄Turn into a parallel stance and execute a straight left punch, right hand guarding.

➤Execute a right punch.

◄Execute a left punch.

➤Execute a right punch.

◁ Execute a left punch and draw the right hand back into the high chambered position.

➤ Rotate left palm up.

◁ Turn into the "circling wrist" block.

➤ Pause in the knife hand position.

◁ Draw the left arm back into the high chambered position.

➤ Draw the right foot to the left, release the tongue from the soft palate.

◁ Exhale through the mouth as you straighten the legs and press down with both palms. Resume normal breathing.

➤ Assume a "relaxed" position.

End of Cham Kiu section.

SECTION THREE

BIU JEE

INTRODUCTION TO SECTION THREE
BIU JEE

Biu Jee is Wing Chun's final "empty hand" set and completes the three basic phases of training. The word "Biu" means to "thrust" and "Jee" means fingers. Hence, the literal translation of Biu Jee is the "thrusting fingers" set. The set is also sometimes called the "flying fingers" set, but "thrusting fingers" is the more common literal translation of the Cantonese.

One could write a complete book on just the Biu Jee set itself. However, my overall goal in this book is to give a brief overview of Wing Chun's three basic "empty hand" sets. Therefore, the Biu Jee set is provided here as a general reference guide for those students who either already know all three sets, or for those students who are currently studying the art from a certified Wing Chun teacher.

When practicing the set, it is important to go slowly at first. You should build-up your speed gradually and only when you have learned to perform the techniques smoothly and with extreme accuracy.

The Biu Jee form focuses on the correct use of the wrist, fingers, and elbows, regaining the center line, and "Point Hitting." By regaining the center line we mean regaining a position of control if your opponent has disrupted your balance or "root" by pushing or pulling you off the center line. In other words, the Biu Jee set teaches one to stay rooted and to maintain a position of "superior advantage" over your opponent. "Point Hitting"—an art that focuses on striking Acupressure points—which can be used in emergency self-defense situations, is also covered in third form training.

Biu Jee Set

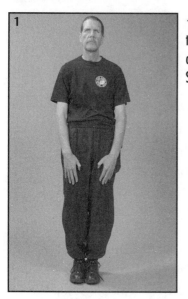

◁ Begin by opening the stance as described at the beginning of Sets #1 and #2.

◄ Place the left fist
on the midline.

➤ Execute a left
straight punch
for the nose.

◁ Snap the fingers open.

➤ Press the fingertips down.

◁ Press the fingertips up.

➤ Press down.

◀Press up.

➤Press down.

◀Press up.

➤Rotate the left hand into the palm-up position.

◄Execute the "circling wrist" block.

➤Keeping the palm facing downwards, sweep the fingers to your right.

◄Sweep the fingers to your left.

➤Sweep the fingers to your right.

◄Sweep
the fingers
to your left.

➤Sweep the fingers
to your right.

◄Sweep the fingers
to your left.

➤Left palm up
position.

◄ "Circling wrist" block.

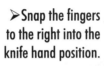

➤ Snap the fingers to the right into the knife hand position.

◄ Withdraw the arm.

Now repeat this same sequence of movements on the right side.

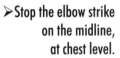 Place the back of the palms together as you turn to your right to execute a left elbow strike.

➤Stop the elbow strike on the midline, at chest level.

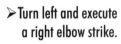 Side view close-up of left elbow strike.

➤Turn left and execute a right elbow strike.

◄ Stop the elbow strike at chest level.

➤ Turn right.

◄ Left elbow strike.

➤ Slide step forward in a right stance and place the back of the right hand under the left elbow.

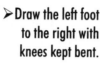 Close-up of elbow and palm positions.

➢ Draw the left foot to the right with knees kept bent.

◄ Shoot out with the right finger thrust to the eyes.

➢ Shoot out with left finger thrust.

◄ Roll the arms through the double "wing block" position.

➤ Draw the arms back into the high chambered position.

◄ Execute a "circle sweep" (counter-clockwise) with the left leg.

➤ Continue the sweep and draw the left leg back into the parallel stance.

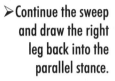 Execute a "circle sweep" (clockwise) with the right leg.

> Continue the sweep and draw the right leg back into the parallel stance.

 "Circle sweep" with the left.

> Draw the left leg back into the parallel stance.

Now repeat this same sequence of movements (the elbow movements and leg sweeps) on the right side.

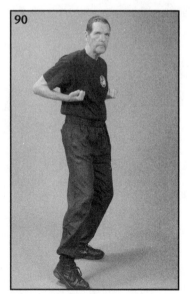

◁ Turn right, left elbow strike.

➢ Withdraw the left arm and execute a right "side palm" strike to the body.

◁ Withdraw the right arm and execute a left "side palm" strike to the body.

➢ Turn into the parallel stance, left hand sweeps through the "horizontal arm" position.

◄ Execute a left "sweeping palm" strike.

➤ Rotate the arm back into the inside palm-up block.

◄ Place the back of the right hand onto the left forearm.

➤ Withdraw the left arm and execute a right vertical palm strike.

100

◁ Rotate right palm up.

101

➢ "Circling wrist" block.

102

◁ Knife hand position.

103

➢ Draw the right arm back into the high chambered position.

Now repeat this same sequence of movements on the right side.

➤Turn right, left elbow strike.

◀◀Execute a right
side palm strike to
the head.

➤Execute a left
side palm strike
to the head.

◀Execute a left
"sweeping arm"
strike.

➤Inside palm-up
block.

◄Right hand
on left forearm.

►Execute a right
vertical palm strike.

◄Rotate right palm up.

►"Circling
wrist" block.

◁ Knife hand position.

◁ Withdraw the right arm into the high chambered position.

Now repeat this same sequence of movements on the right side.

➤ Execute an upward "sweeping hand" strike to the left side as the right hand slap blocks.

138

◁ Now, sweep right.

139

▷ Sweep left, again.

140

◁ Inside left palm-up block.

141

▷ Turn left and execute a left hand "circle wrist" block.

◄ Turn back,
left inside
palm-up
block.

➤ Turn left,
"circle wrist"
block.

◄ Turn back,
left inside
palm-up block.

➤ Turn left, "circle
wrist" block.

146

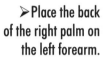

◄ Turn back,
left inside
palm-up block.

➤ Place the back
of the right palm on
the left forearm.

147

148

◄ Execute a right
vertical palm strike.

➤ Rotate right
palm up.

149

 "Circling wrist" block.

➤ Knife hand position.

◄ Withdraw right arm into the high chambered position.

Now repeat this same sequence of movements on the right side.

◁ Turn the stance 45° to the left and execute a simultaneous right inside palm-up block and a left palm-down ("double hand" block).

➤ Turn right, right "double hand" block.

◁ Turn left, left "double hand" block.

➤ Turn back into inside palm-up block.

◄ Right palm
on left forearm.

➤ Right vertical
palm strike.

◄ Rotate right
palm up.

➤ "Circling wrist"
block.

◁ Knife hand position.

◁ Withdraw right arm into the high chambered position.

Now repeat this same sequence of movements on the right side.

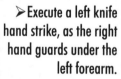 Sink the left elbow into "pulling hand" block.

➤ Execute a left knife hand strike, as the right hand guards under the left forearm.

◄Sweep right hand up into a knife hand strike.

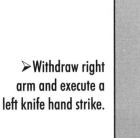

➤Withdraw right arm and execute a left knife hand strike.

◄Turn right and execute an inside palm-up block.

➤Thrust the arm forward into a left "side palm" position.

◄ Turn back
and execute a left
upward "sweeping
hand" strike.

➤ Inside left
palm-up block.

◄ Right palm
on left forearm.

➤ Right vertical
palm strike.

◄ Rotate right palm up.

➤ "Circling wrist" block.

◄ Knife hand position.

➤ Withdraw right arm into the high chambered position.

Now repeat this same sequence of movements on the right side.

◁ Open hands and execute a vertical "double palm" strike at chest level.

➤ Execute a "double grab" (make two fists, palms turned downwards)

◁ Turn to the left, maintaining the "double grab" position.

➤ Withdraw the right arm as you make a "middle knuckle" fist with the left hand.

◁ Rotate the body back into the parallel stance and execute a left "middle knuckle" strike.

➤ Inside left palm-up block.

223

◄ Execute an left "inverted palm" strike to the body.

➤ Rotate the left palm up.

224

225

⋏ "Circling wrist" block.

226

⋏ Knife hand position.

227

⋏ Withdraw left arm.

Now repeat this same sequence of movements on the right side.

> Press both palms
together into the
double "prayer
hand" position.

240

◄Bend forward and down, pressing the hands between the legs.

241

➤Sweep the hands upwards.

242

◄Continue sweeping the hands upwards and bring them over the back of the head.

243

➤Separate the palms.

◁ Draw the arms to the sides.

➤ Make two fists and assume the left guard position.

◁ Execute a left punch.

➤ Right punch.

◄ Left punch.

➤ Right punch.

◄ Left punch and withdraw the right arm.

➤ Rotate left palm up.

◄ "Circling wrist" block.

➤ Knife hand position.

◄ Withdraw left arm into the high chambered position.

➤ Draw the left leg to the right.

◁ Straighten the legs and press down with both palms as you exhale.

▷ Relax the body and begin to breathe normally.

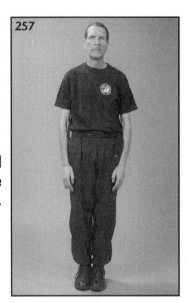

End of Biu Jee section.

Section Four

Form Techniques and Applications

First Form Applications

⋏Lori applies basic left "slap block" to "outside" of Ziv's right punch.

⋏Lori's block has the potential to extend into an outside finger jab to Ziv's neck (following the Wing Chun maxim "all blocks can be strikes, and all strikes can be blocks").

⋏Lori applies basic palm-up block to "inside" of Ziv's right punch.

⋏Again, this palm-up block has the potential to extend into an "inside" finger jab.

⋏Lori applies basic "slap block" to the "inside" of Ziv's right punch.

⋏Lori uses a palm strike/deflection attack to counter Ziv's left punch.

⋏Ziv grabs Lori's left arm.

⋏Lori counters with a simultaneous left palm-down block and right punch to Ziv's head.

Second Form Applications

Lap Sau or "Grabbing Hand" Drill

The basic techniques for the Lap Sau drill are taken directly from the Cham Kiu Set. Although the techniques are demonstrated from the parallel stance, the Lap Sau drill can also be performed with the stance and body turned at 45.°

◄ Begin the drill with the left forearms crossed.

◄ Ziv pulls down Lori's left arm and executes a right punch.

◄ Lori protects with a high left "wing block."

◄ Now Lori pulls down Ziv's right arm, maintaining forward pressure with her grabbing hand.

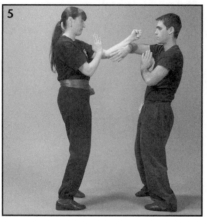

◁ Ziv protects with a high right "wing block." At this point, Ziv has two options. He can either return the grab and punch sequence or, as shown, change sides by applying the simultaneous palm-up block and punch. There are many "changes" contained within the basic "grabbing hand" drill.

◁ Ziv changes punching attack to the opposite side.

◁ Now Lori protects herself by applying a right "wing block."

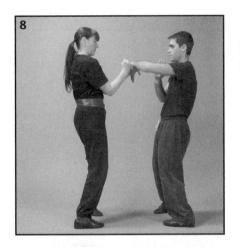

◁ Lori could change sides but, as shown, pulls down Ziv's left arm and executes a right punch.

◁ Ziv protects himself with a left "wing block" and is then ready to recycle the drill.

Second Form Applications (Continued)

◄ Lori applies a left "slap block" to "outside" of Ziv's right punch.

◄ Her "slap block" transitions into a "reverse wing block" around Ziv's arm.

◄ She now pivots and simultaneously attacks Ziv's head with a right counter punch.

◅ Lori blocks Ziv's grab with a "double" bent wrist block.

◅ She applies a double "grabbing hand" block to control Ziv's arms.

◅ Lori finishes with a front kick to Ziv's body.

Third Form Applications

⋀ Chris faces Sifu Lamb in a right guarding position.

⋀ Sifu Lamb attacks with a left "slap block" and right eye jab.

⋀ Chris protects with a left "slap block."

⋀ Sifu Lamb immediately counters Chris's block with a second eye jab attack.

⋏He finishes off with a knife hand strike to the throat.

⋏Sifu Lamb attacks with a left "slap block" and right eye jab.

⋏He controls Chris's right arm with an outside "grabbing hand" block.

⋏Next, he drives a left palm into Chris's waist.

⋏Sifu Lamb now controls Chris's left arm and drives a "Third Form" elbow strike into his chest.

⋏Sifu Lamb finishes by turning his right arm into an "upward" elbow strike to Chris's throat.

⋏Sifu Lamb attacks Chris with a right "deflecting" eye jab strike.

⋏He then grabs Chris's right arm.

◁ Next he executes a left "upward" elbow break.

◁ Sifu Lamb steps back with the left foot and drives a right knife hand into Chris's waist.

◁ He finishes with a strong right side kick to the body.

Third Form Applications (Continued)

⏶Quang faces Sifu Lamb in a right guarding stance.

⏶Sifu Lamb applies a left grab to Quang's right punch and counters with a right side palm strike to the head.

⏶Lamb continues with a right elbow strike.

⏶"Neck pull" attack.

⋏Sifu Lamb combines the "neck pull" with a leg sweep takedown.

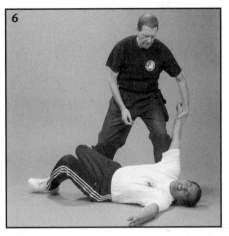

⋏He continues into an arm and shoulder lock.

⋏Quang faces Sifu Lamb in a right guarding stance.

⋏Quang initiates with a right punch.

⋏Sifu Lamb uses a left finger jab to defect the punch.

⋏Quang throws a right punch.

⋏This time, Sifu Lamb thrusts out with his right arm, deflecting Quang's right punch.

⋏Sifu Lamb extends his right arm into a right eye jab.

Third Form Applications (Continued)

◄ Quang initiates with a right punch.

◄ Sifu Lamb applies a left "slap block" to the "outside" of Quang's right punch.

◄ Using a "running hand" technique, Lamb jabs his fingers into Quang's eyes.

Third Form Flow Drill

⚔Lori and Ziv face each other in a parallel stance, left arms crossed.

⚔Lori checks Ziv's left arm with her right and executes a left elbow strike. Ziv stops the elbow attack with a right palm-up block.

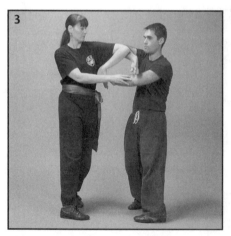

⚔Ziv now uses a right "wing block" to deflect Lori's attack.

⚔Ziv uses his left hand to maintain control over Lori's elbow.

⋏Ziv uses a right "upward" elbow strike to attack Lori's left arm.

⋏Ziv applies a reverse "wing block" to sweep Lori's arm to his right, and sets up to attack with his left arm.

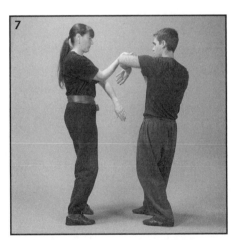

⋏Ziv executes a left elbow strike and Lori protects with her left palm-up block.

⋏Lori uses her right "wing block" to deflect Ziv's elbow attack.

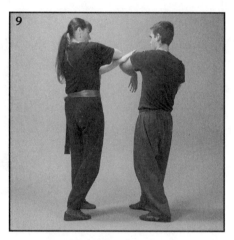

⋏Lori uses her left hand to control
Ziv's elbow.

⋏Lori applies an "upward" elbow attack
to Ziv's arm.

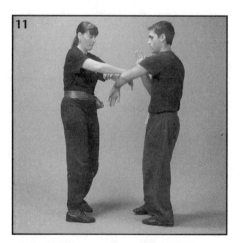

⋏Lori applies a reverse "wing block" sweep.

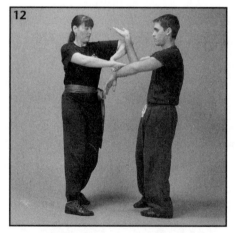

⋏Lori again attacks with her left elbow,
starting the drill over again. The drill is
then recycled back and forth.

Combat Application of Third Form Flow Drill
Illustration of "Elbow Break" Technique

⋏ Ziv begins an attack with his right arm.

⋏ Lori deflects the blow with a left "wing block."

⋏ Lori applies an arm-break defense.

⋏ She uses her left reverse "wing block" to deflect Ziv's arm and simultaneously attacks Ziv's jaw with a right palm strike.

◁ Lori sinks her right elbow.

◁ Then attacks Ziv with a right elbow strike.

◁ Lori finishes with a knife hand strike to Ziv's throat.

CONCLUSION

I hope you have enjoyed this volume of Explosive Combat Wing Chun. I have demonstrated the three sets the way they were taught to me in Hong Kong by my last Sifu, Koo Sang. Always remember that the sets may vary slightly from school to school but that, structurally, there should be little variation. Your main focus as regards the forms should be to master an understanding of basic structure. Additionally, an emphasis on correct body and hand positions are important so that when you need to apply techniques in a combat situation, you will have no doubt as to the correct angle or proper hand position for any technique.

Wing Chun is a high maintenance art. Having said that, although practitioners seldom forget how to instinctively apply the techniques once they have learned the basics, remaining sharp requires not only a thorough understanding of all three forms and their structure, but continuous practice and refinement. Therefore, you should not look at the forms as something to be "learned" so that you can move on to other things—e.g., Chi Sau, sparring, etc.—but rather you should understand that continuous and correct practice of all three forms is linked to the correct execution of technique.

The world situation as of late has shown that we need to be able to protect ourselves and others at a moment's notice. That is why I believe it is more important now than ever for the average citizen to study some form of martial arts. Having said that, I also believe that martial arts has a lot more to offer than just self-defense. Self-confidence, self-respect, health, well-being, balance, spiritual awareness, philosophy, and psychology are all areas that martial arts training allows us to explore. When it comes to martial arts training, "dig deep," look below the surface. It's not all just about kicking or punching. If you approach your martial arts training with this attitude, not only will you be able to develop a deeper understanding of whatever style you choose, but you will also find that your training will be much more rewarding.

In closing, always remember that as martial artists we generally are—and should be—held to a higher standard. Therefore, I ask those of you with high level martial arts skills to act responsibly. I think it is important for martial artists to keep a sense of balance and not to become egotists focused solely on fighting. This is a challenge given that you are striving to develop superior fighting skills and many times will find yourself in a situation where you know you can easily beat an opponent. However, try to remember that Kung-Fu was developed by Buddhist monks primarily as a means of self-defense, not as a means to harm those who are weaker. Unless your life is being threatened, try to avoid using your skills to hurt others. It is always best to walk away from a fight if you can because, if you injure someone, you could be facing a lawsuit, or someone hell-bent on revenge. Use whatever force is necessary to protect yourself, but act intelligently.

Good luck with your training.

ABOUT THE AUTHOR

Alan Lamb is England's first Hong Kong trained Master of Wing Chun. He has been involved in the martial arts for over 30 years, beginning first with the Wado Ryu style of Karate, and later turning to Wing Chun Kung-Fu, which he has practiced for over twenty-five years. For several years he studied in London under Sifu Paul Lam, a prominent teacher of Wing Chun in England. Later he studied with Sifu Joseph Cheng, also in London. Subsequently, he was accepted for a year long instructor's course in Hong Kong under Master Koo Sang, a direct disciple of Yip Man, the Grand Master of Wing Chun Kung-Fu. During his stay in Hong Kong, Malaysia and Singapore, Lamb also studied some miscellaneous aspects of the Siu Lum Ji with Sifu Wong Wan Chin, a Shaolin monk. Later, he studied Filipino martial arts with several teachers, including Professor Vee of New York.

In 1974 Lamb graduated from Mr. Koo's academy and earned the title Sifu ("teacher") of Wing Chun Kung-Fu.

He later established schools in both England and the United States and is presently teaching a select group of students in California.

Sifu Lamb is also concentrating on promoting the art of Wing Chun through movies and television. He has demonstrated his art in England, Hong Kong, the United States, and Latin America, as well as making a special guest appearance in "The Oriental World of Self Defense" at Madison Square Garden.

Anyone who is interested in studying personally with Sifu Lamb can contact him through the publishers.